PRAISE FOR WALTE

"In the Belly of the Beast", lik(of these elegant and fiercely imagined prose poems revivifies a biblical myth by the most direct and comic method available by taking it literally. Here is Jonah "frantically plugging the leaks, mopping his invisible floor. . .ready to throw in the towel," and here he is "kicking at the debris of civilizations." In the process Jonah comes to stand for us all.

— Tom Andrews
judge for *Quarter After Eight* Prize

[*The Feast*] is hugely ambitious, original, affecting, and at many points, extraordinarily powerful.

— *St. Louis Post-Dispatch*

Each time I dive into Bargen's fractured world of legend and art, I find my heart strangely warmer and my mind slightly fuller "as if" as the author states in "Born Under Glass", "excruciating details were our only certainties.

— *Sentence*

History is not a nightmare from which Bargen is trying to awake; it is a sea of contingency, congruence, and limitless possibility into which Bargen dives headlong.

— Gary Young

Walter Bargen regularly fulfills the mission of making visible (and sensible) things that are either too humble to be noticed or too familiar to remind us of their remarkable being without the help of Bargen's sharp eye and often startling wit.

— *Pleiades*

…these poems are not staged shockers…They contain genuine feeling and each is a subtle, cautionary deliverance.

— *The Georgia Review*

AND PRAISE FOR *UNTIL NEXT TIME*

After a poet's twenty-second book, a reader might expect (and even forgive) repetition—of style, theme, turn of phrase. The surprising thing in *Until Next Time* by Walter Bargen is that everywhere this poet looks, he does so with fresh eyes: Everything he sees, he sees new—"as if wonder / comes to us for the first time, flanked / by driftwood." Keen political insights couple with close observation of the ordinary and natural world to create poems of unusual—but not unexpected—breadth. For fans of Bargen's work, this collection is another vivid bead on the strand.

—Karen Craigo, *Passing Through Humansville* and *No More Milk*

A glance at the titles of the poems in Walter Bargen's *Until Next Time* let's the readers know we are at sea or up a creek and out in the rain in his watery visions. These poems set us pondering life on the coast of action or treading water amidst the flume and flow. They take us to the center of our universes, out to "where we swim each day, risking riptides." The pathways and pondings of water lace the world, and *Until Next Time* is an expedition among those many destinations.

—Clarence Wolfshohl, *Chupacabra* and *Queries & Wonderments*

UNTIL NEXT TIME

WALTER BARGEN

Cover Art and Cover Design: Michael Sleadd

Library of Congress Control Number 2019947872

ISBN 978-0-9334392-0-7

Singing Bone Press

Columbia, SC

www.singingbonepress.com

Dedication

For family and friends who, again and again, draw me West, especially, the Pacific Northwest:

Kale, Elizabeth, Rowan Fox Rose-White, and Cedar;

Joyce and Alan Berner;

Reggie and Steve Tackett-Nelson;

Candy and Tom Clardy.

Another heart-felt thank you to Matt Dube for reading an early version of this manuscript.

And huge heart-felt thanks to the artist Michael Sleadd for yet another spectacular book cover.

ACKNOWLEDGMENTS

Cover Art and Cover Design by Michael Sheadd

These poems first appeared in

Big Muddy — Everything Exists in Its Own Imperfection
The Broadkill Review — Coastal (Sections 1-2, 4-7)
Cavalier Magazine — Natural Causes
Cleaver — Bye, Bye Olduvai
Mare Tranquilltatus
Cuivre River — Staying With Friends
Elder Mountain — By Now
Flint Hills Review — Day After the Election
Gingko Tree Review — Trolling
Altitude Sickness
I-70 Review — A Mouse of Trouble
Kansas City Star — Forgotten History
MARGIE — Leafing Town
Miramir — Geography Bull
Point Dume Screen Test
Mochilla Review — Babylonian Moment
Permafrost — The Untamed
Poetrymagazine.com — San Francisco
Volcanic Fields
Redactions — Coastal Limits
Coastal Risk
Coastal Discarded
River Styx — Photographing the Wind
San Pedro River Review — Volunteer Park
Directions of Rain
The Cape Rock — Bench Sitter
Thirteen Miles from Cleveland — Winged Life
Valpariso Review — Prague Flood
Vox Populi — Midwest Estate Sale
Old Rain
Interruption to the End

Quotations from Chief Seattle are from "Chief Seattle's 1854 Oration," first reported in a column by Dr. Henry A. Smith, Seattle Sunday Star, October 29, 1887. The authenticity of this oration is questioned by some historians.

"Everything Exists in Its own Imperfection" is from the book, *Gone West*, published by Illiom-Verlag, Germany, 2014.

"Parental Advice" appears in the anthology New Century North American Poets, River King Poetry Press, 2002.

"Angola to Zanzibar" appears in the anthology Knowing Stones: Poems of Exotic Places, John Gordon Publisher, Inc., 2000.

"Abject Impermanence in Kansas," appears in Begin Again: 150 Kansas Poems, Woodley Memorial Press, 2011.

"Photographing the Wind" appears in the book, Remedies for Veritgo, Cherry Grove Editions, 2006.

"A Distant Theory" appears in the letterpress book, Three-Corner Catch, Grito del Lobo Press, 2015, a poetic conversation with Clarence Wolfshohl

Until Next Time

1

2

Coastal

3

4

5

Refuse

Along the Way

A careless pilgrim scatters the dust of his passions more widely.

—Dhammapada

I didn't tell all I saw, because no one would have believed me.

— Marco Polo

People don't have your past to hold against you. No yesterdays on the road.

—William Least-Heat Moon

Traveler there is no path. Paths are made by walking.

—Antonio Machado

Mapping terrain where we have never been,
The landscape of the country of our blindness.

—Herbert Morris

The feel of *location* of being just where I am and nowhere else is unendurable.

—William Burroughs

1

Even the rocks, which seem to be dumb and dead as they swelter in the sun along the silent shore, thrill with memories . . . .

—Chief Seattle

Old Rain

Up down, up down, no pause, no let up in the falling.
Ovate, serrate, oblong, lobed, green scales weighing
each droplet then bending into the fall. A full sky yet
     to weigh.
At the foot of each leaf a puddle taps out time.

Not Enough Sky

The sky, variations on perfection:
the north-south bridge softening into evening,
Cascade peaks no longer jagged.
West, snow-streaked Olympics.
Below the sun's orange crush,
the Sound's slate slush begins to well up.

    Once Salish canoes paddled these salt waterways.
Once the sky was too low.
Once fish hawks grew tired of walking.
People tired of bending over,
banging their heads trying to stand.
Their backs hurt.
Smoke flattened over cooking fires
was always in the way of seeing
who sat on the other side.

An erratic ant travels the concrete
railing of the undrawn bridge.
What else is there?
Heavy gears wait to turn
for the high-masted boats
of the rich, lifting the road
and pouring traffic into the sky.

The Salish who climbed fir trees
disappeared into the airy world.
Mothers cried when they saw
their lost children flying
far out of reach. They cut
their long black braids to make a rope
to tie down their losses.

Fifty feet below the rusting railing,
the opaque green channel,
where fifty-foot-long boats trail
pale, propeller-churned wakes.
My Fair Lady nudges past Nest Egg,
their waves chattering against the stained,
graffitied concrete sea walls.

The Salish elders called the many peoples together:
the ravens, the seals, the woodpeckers,
any tribe that could hold a long pole.
They pushed and each time
the sky backed off a few inches.

Two kingfishers dip down and fly,
under the bridge girders
that hum with the flood of tires
crossing steel grates.

When the sky was high enough
the Salish, no longer blinded by smoke,
stopped tripping over scavenging crows.
They'd been careful not to poke
holes in the sky, but when darkness arrived,
there were thousands of lights shining
through night's skin to remind them
of a world pushed away, stolen,
to traffic in this one.

A Path Is Made By Walking

—for Mike Sleadd

Surely, this is one of the nearly extinct

avian citizens that never existed,

who never soared over the uprising

of this great city, but finds itself satisfied

to walk on three legs through

vast wilderness parks, strolling

around its wide lakes that reflect

the high stories of buildings shouting tales

of ascendance, its broad boulevards kept

meticulously clean of the debris that is

passed down from generation to generation.

So nothing new is expected as all

the exceptions are quickly deposited

in every street corner receptacle,

all the exclusions quickly excluded

so all the street signs are removed,

all directions inclusive of all other directions,

all the incongruities quickly worked into

the design of the next monumental

construction project, and all the contradictions

cancelling out further contradictions,

lost and found identical, leaving the city

a heap of rubble and this avian citizen alone

and lonely walks to the city limits toward

the destruction of the next improbable city.

Once Across

1

Three mallards paddle toward the iron railing.
Its intricate cross-hatched shadows
stitch the waves,
quilt the wakes of boats.

A work day and the mallards wait to be fed.
I break a granola bar into pieces.
Two ducks paddle a short distance back,
refusing to join in the bad behavior of one duck.

Stream-lined, torpedo-slick, fiber-glass hulls
chop the green water, lifting
and dropping three feathered buoys
that are surfing their daily hungers.

A seaplane drones overhead, a skillsaw screeches
through a cut inside a nearby house,
the I-5 bridge continues to hurtle traffic
north and south through a city that daily turns
itself inside out. The water wavers composing
a light overture but never slows down.

2

The crow's shadow
      darker than the crow.
Water deepens to obsidian
      as it flies past.

A loose tailpipe
      is dragged over asphalt,
late sun throws up sparks
      igniting the bridge's
concrete underbelly.

Flash of pale blades—
      kayaks hug the seawall
and brilliantly slice the channel.

In the bay, boats tack
      in slow motion,
lifeless laundry
      lost to its body of wind.

The white-flared parentheses of gulls

      fly past as if everything

in this city is a hungry

      afterthought.

Evening enters us.

      We dine on scarlet clouds.

Marbled waters drain to pastel.

      Motorboats disappear

into the sky.

Either Way

From the bedroom, I stare
        at miles of fogged Pacific Coast.
The white scarred waves mark
        the wound that never heals,
that totals on the shore the detritus,
        the once-lived, the half-alive.

Sea star, crab, mussels grind
        together into a new life.
Last night Cassiopeia sat
        in her stellar chair.
The Big Dipper drunk poured
        a vast emptiness.

Streaked dome—two bits
        of celestial debris
burn out, too-quick
        for my too slow wishes.
Barely visible, the salted glitter of a town
        marks the bay's far turning.
Pinprick of blood, lemon slice,
        hydrangea, balls of rhododendron—
a far away festival's muted fireworks

bloom over the ocean's turbulent palm.

Waves' echoes drag us

back to the living, then back to the dead.

Rain

He walks through aromas spilling
from coffee shops on Ninth,

past the stale odors of overstocked used bookstores
and the musty second-hand clothing stores.

He sees the sidewalk drizzle-sheen
always a couple of reflections away—

a coin that keeps rolling out of reach, heads
or tails, his luck always a step or two ahead.

Midwest Estate Sale

Tape secures tattered strips of paper
with hand-written prices:
paperbacks fifty cents, hardbacks $2,
linen chest $175, ten-disk cd changer $40,
and a cassette player that I buy for $3,
along with a 4-drawer filing cabinet,
but it's the stampless, addressless,
unwritten postcards that I return to,
their ninety-year-old panoramic vistas pristine,
photographs painted for color: Puget Sound a blue
it's never known, a Seattle waterfront
of ten-story buildings, never so clear and clean again,
the shot taken from over the harbor in an aeroplane,
and headed out of the picture the slick-ball, art-deco,
silver-lined *Kalakala* ferry, leaving the white
scar of its wake cutting for Bremerton before it sailed
to Alaska, up the Yukon River to haul mining
equipment to get-rich-quick claims that played out
too quickly, the ferry scuttled on a sandbar scoured
by sandpipers. Decades later it's towed back
to Seattle, brought through Government Locks,
to be reclaimed, refurbished, renovated,
but left as a bankrupt rusting hulk

in the shadows of the Aurora Bridge.

How often do we get dragged back

only to find out what was unfinished,

unfixable, unwanted is still so?

The locks on Government Canal another postcard,

claiming to be second only to the Panama Canal

in ship-size carried, lifting hulls from Puget Sound

to Lake Union. What's locked and unlocked is

only glimpsed in the quick-moving murky current.

When I ask the price for the postcards,

the dead man's sister turns to me and says

that I look familiar, did I know her brother,

he sold siding, the garage and shed

crammed with samples, all for sale.

He was a bachelor: it's there in the boxes of books

between Timothy Leary and *Storming Heaven*,

a sexual bliss manual and how to meet the perfect

woman, and later at home, after I watch one

of the dvds from the box, *Edward Scissorhands*,

that he'd downloaded from satellite, there at the end

a half minute of fellatio between a hard-working
woman and a laid-back well-endowed man.

Divorced, she says, and perhaps that gave
him hours to learn bank shots
on the pool table downstairs that's already
sold. There's *A Hundred Years of Solitude*, also
on my list of ten best books of the twentieth century.
There's Lars Gustafsson's *Death of a Beekeeper*,
another author in my pantheon. Yes, I think
I knew him. His sister looks more familiar each time
I ask her a question. I'm afraid to see a picture.
I don't want another person that I almost knew.
There are already haunted multitudes in my life.
In the basement, I find a parsons table and buy it.
His nephew helps me carry it to the car through a cold
April rain. His uncle died almost being known.

Gold Boat from the Broighter Hoard

We journey in business, economy,
steerage, stowaway, or on a gold boat
outfitted with a lightly notched rim for rowlocks,
two rows of nine long oars thin as reeds,
this a millennium-old, seven-inch vessel,
all that's needed to ferry a soul.

The rudder locked in a predistined direction,
headed away from where most of us
would rather be, even back into a 1896 field
behind the horse-drawn plow that strikes
the nondescript mud-encrusted metal lump.
A gold soul washed clean by a maid
who decries pieces lost down the drain.

Explanations abound, flooding a river:
winged disk of an Egyptian barge afloat
over desert light, dragon-bowed Viking ship
fired and sinking toward Valhalla,
Irish Iron Age golden boat, a votive
for the sea god Manannán mac Lir,
its small weight enough to raise the water

to reach the other shore where circles
of paradise and hell tangle. Yet we return
to the same dirt and detritus, rusty bottle caps
from aborted vacations and the sharp glitter
of splintered glass, all that has escaped
our shortened attention spans

and the weight of all our inattentions.
Above where the keel might have crossed the hull
of the gleaming bowl, a spindly stick mast rises,
last hope for favorable winds to sail us easily
into our deaths, absolving us of the back-breaking
labor of an invisible crew sweating on gold benches.

The port of call calling with its incessant and ecstatic
music, banshees and angels in Celtic swirls along
the beach, the manic beat enough to raise the dead
to dance in ragged lines, and now all we have to do
is jump the gunwale, wade ashore, expect nothing
then to meet our golden souls.

Brown Pelican, Vashon Island

—after a photograph by Alan Berner

Before it was simply recording, framing facts,
                not time as much as the times
in time, certainly not the still-point of time's negation
                sitting on this porch late Sunday morning,
late implying more than was meant, an admonishment
                of the passing, a fracturing of futures,

not a longing for elsewhere, where late is just another
                angle of light, another spin and wobble of
a planet. A day of perfect warmth erases limits, giving
                up the soft edges of body for the softer air,
where I dissolve into the yard into the chin-high
                asparagus plumes that sift the heat through

the garden, green Egyptian slaves deep in the temple
                fanning their sun god, and there on the other
side of the field another self about to walk into the shifting
                shadows of oaks, and there too at the horizon
about to take one step beyond the past, I'm everywhere
                at once simply following my shifting stare

until my eyelids shut and then I'm beyond beyond, even

this simple passing where the skin of air
that is my skin brushes the magenta milkweed stage
where its troupe of flowers slowly spin
at the end of a lanky stalk that passes without
a scratch through the woven wire fence

topped with a single strand of barb-wire, petals
that blow gently against the hedge
of cedars, inflaming their darkness under near-noon
light, as oak leaves surrender the house
rising in its own tide, waves attached to branches,
the susurrations of a beach covered

with the flamboyant punctuations of umbrellas,
emphatic with nothing more to say,
hyphenated with the cotton dashes of spread towels
facing off where sky and sea merge.
This saintly penetration of all things, until the shutter
stopped time over the mercurial water

with a pair of half-folded wings, more like crutches
mangled by a bully in the glory of his
weakness, and a pair of webbed feet sticking straight
out from a cartoon round white belly
and into the equally improbable salty air, useless

in any event for paddling through

in the nanosecond left of this rapturous dive,

following its long neck, contorted

as a plumbing diagram, following the shovel-blade

of its long beak as it begins to leave

one world and enter another, the wet membrane

undeniable, unavoidable, opening,

opening. That's all it will do, the pelican left

pirouetting on a wave-slack sea,

the fish flash fading if not lost, time sculpted still

in the turning, as I turn the photograph

upside down to see the other miracle

of diving into a sea of sky.

Rain

He has plans: arrivals and departures,
appointments at three dumpsters,

ready to ignore what he hears about who
and what, ready to ignore the advice

of those who keep getting it wrong and don't
stop bragging about it. Getting it right

is the future, his plastic bag bulging with empty
beer cans, the metallic rain of the promised land.

Bench Sitter

I don't know if you lived in this city your entire life,
or what occupied your time, a job in finance most like-
ly, lumberjack unimaginable, your so-called free time
surely involved something larger than a boat,
or what you or others consider your accomplishments,
enough to memorialize this bench with an envelope-
sized brass plaque, one that could conceal a personal
letter, though that matters little to you I think, or if life
goes on this gesture is a subterfuge to cover up your
living disappearance, and then it really was you
who left the carry-out barbeque sauce containers
filled with rainwater under the bench where I sit over-
looking Azalea Way.

It is too early or too late for the froth of blooms
that carpet the well-groomed mulch beds that are
heaped high like fresh graves until the dirt and dust
settles into tranquil mowable lawn. After a lifetime of
seeing the inward collapse under the weight of silence,
I'm not certain of the timing, letting you know
that I'm just passing through, how a week here

and there has left me on your bench in the Arboretum

trying to sort out the clouds into phylum and species as

they all run in one direction, away, as if they know

something, or were spooked and headed for the edge

that you'd already found, falling toward the horizon,

but then slipping into the endless curve of space,

that leaves a bench lichen and moss occupied.

Everything Exists in its Own Imperfection

Without imperfection, neither you nor I would exist.

—Stephen Hawking

The West was in us. I don't know what happened.
Cochise and Kit Carson, Seattle and San Francisco,
saguaro and redwood, ocotillo and Douglas fir.
More absolute, intense and pure.
More dust than blood. More basalt than bone.
And never enough sky. We were sure of that.
Clouds stepping beyond what we knew
and where we prayed to arrive.

I can't claim forty years is a long time,
but it is, and once, arms out-stretched,
crucified by an uninterrupted light,
pirouetting upward on the roof
of the Kiwanis stone shelter on Sandia Ridge,
ten thousand feet to fall if I wanted,
and I did, and some of us have.

Mt. Taylor far into the western sun,
the southern spine of the Manzanos
purpling into dusk, the Sangre de Cristos

bleeding rock through another disiccated evening,

and to the east, drawn outward a hundred miles,

my shadow prospects for disappearance.

2

A few more moons, a few more winters . . . .

—Chief Seattle

Coastal

Coastal Fable

Slate smooth, blue silhouette, fading definitions.
Sun candles the city skyline and distant
mountain peaks. The final blush: mists

mingle, rise. Dogs bark an unrehearsed
chorus. Long throated highways
devour ceaseless traffic.

Under a backyard lamp, dragonflies
sweep low over garden pools. Mottled
goldfish kiss the surface, their round

mouths begging for something in return.
Not this time, we are too busy
listening to gunshots blocks away.

Coastal: the last ships pass, the bridges
draw closed. Across bays, tree-lined banks,
side streets, valleys are reunited by one more night.

Lights braid the water. None of us

can believe this, then we forget and do,

the city full sail, headed for the Pacific.

Coastal Risk

North, a man is reported shot in his car.
The headline reads "Parked Forever."
A small town has its first tabloid death:

windshield a vast star-cracked map,
the shatterproof diagram with one small black
hole, no motive but advanced alien technology.

In the next town south, a man is found face down,
arms outstretched on his front lawn,
embracing grass, the journey work of stars,

his body naked and desperately mutilated.
The motive headlined, "Love Affair Severed."
This is what you find coastal:

the range road dropping precipitously,
folding back on itself, leading nowhere
but into a series of turns that threaten to turn

into a hang knot of asphalt. This year eight deaths
on this stretch of highway: some simply
dizzy with switchbacks, some drunk on salt

spray, some lost in visions of towering

Douglas fir, some played out at reservation casinos,

all having lost the lives they invented.

Coastal Limits

South, tractors turn in clouds
of dust, their deep-cleated tires disappearing
and reappearing, as if black rubber

were ratcheting the earth in directions
other than rotations and revolutions.
Harrowing: mere magic, mundane

sleight-of-hand, the turning of fields.
Vast networks of irrigation, sprinklers
throw out shimmering plumes, wings

of wet light, the glancing fractures
of a low-angled sun. Over the coastal range
the ocean is furrowing wave after mindless wave.

Coastal Accounting

In the Fremont District,
the garbage truck's backup-warning bell
is the morning alarm, though the hammering

at the end of the block demands
an accounting. All employ a similar swing:
remodeling, demolition, break-in, fight.

The same vector for deliverance and destruction.
A carpenter sleeps in the bushes
in the median, wrapped in yesterday's economic

boom, society's notables, and get-rich-quick want ads.
A gull flies over roofs headed toward the channel.
Another pumps the damp air in the opposite

direction. The mystery of sirens
on a gale-swept rocky shore attracts us,
inviting us to come crash, though others have

already driven into a concrete traffic barrier,
brick wall, bridge abutment, or sailed off
a shoulder into the bay with the cormorants.

Our last moments of sleep confused,
reliving our cherished accidents,
that choking heroic gasp before waking.

Coastal Discarded

Facing north into Puget Sound,
benched pigeons pump their heads and coo
having survived another day on the discarded.

Waves unzip the shore.
The restless rubble of shells
and civilizations wash in and out.

Gulls mob a girl tossing bread, unhinging
their madhouse shrieks when their beaks
go empty.

By the seawall a plume of spray
runs up the eroding concrete steps.
Sun smears the air

then drains down, returning
to the broader glitter of the Sound.
Sweatered, a few bent men sit most

of the afternoon, eating sandwiches
out of paper bags, playing chess,
staring at the occasional freighter,

counting the wakes' waves following
the hourly island ferries. Evening,
they walk their small steps, over the scattered,

the broken, over wet sand, through a corrosive
yellow light, past old-pigeoned women cooing
of better days and knowing better.

Coastal Backyard

A float plane flies low, merges
with its choppy shadow on small choppy waves,
leaving a winged thing floating on turbulent

green, a bobbing metal leaf that leaves
gulls alone to attend to evening strollers
stopped to lean on the crumbling seawall.

Evening settles the city. They watch the passing
motor launch sporting the exclamations of blue-buoyed
gunwales. The wake of receding light

turns lanky far-shore buildings into trembling
silvered slivers, quivering smears, soon dulled
and dissolving. The bridges draw up,

the homeless return to doorways,
to tunnels warmed by exhaust,
affixed to another night.

Coastal Mourning

These last mornings are easiest
where weeks of regret resolve.
Consolation an uninterrupted

horizon. Street to street, power line
intersecting power line, mark no more than
this place, the "x" that marks the living.

A gray cat walks the sidewalk as it has
for years. Minutes later a yellow tabby patrols
in the opposite direction, timed to meet

only scents, shadows, the faint tale of strangers.
Last night the city spread its own version of the starry
sky over the bay. Lights bubbled down

the hillsides as we descended and drowned,
but we went down only once.
Paler morning fated east, sea turning inside

sea beyond the bleached houses,
the unseen couple strolls the foggy beach, their next
step where the gulls and sandpipers take flight.

Coastal Shipwreck

We arrive at innocence, as if we never longed
for this winded beach, this cloud-strafed sky,
to find a way to breathe salt water again.

The gulls evenly spaced along the half-submerged log,
what's left from last night's storm, pretend
to abandon their customary calculations,

the day's hungers, their cranky voices,
their beggarly dispositions. As if wonder
comes to us for the first time, flanked

by driftwood, we glimpse in the breaking
sea fog something a half mile out,
something so large and on a collision

course with our end of the beach, that we sit
astounded, stupefied, catatonic, until the fog shifts
south and our monstrous-hulled ship clears

into a ragged sea stack colliding with waves,
its port of call already eroded into pieces.
Translucent anemones, orange sea-stars

pooled by ebb tides, born on each volley of surf,
each plumed spray. Buried in the shadows
of dunes, the day's thin pulse reddens

along the Pacific's far edge. We grieve
with the past left ahead of us
and our future behind.

Coastal Wash

The coast crying out for tragedy like all beautiful places.

—Robinson Jeffers

(for Kale and Elizabeth and Bobette)

After the hammer crash of the churning crest
What's left of the wave thrashes on the shore
As if some shy, fearful thing from the deep,
Shocked by the salt-stormed air, wants back under.

The wave draws down and rounded pebbles
Follow its ebbing leash amid bone rattle
And shell clatter, leaving the polished granite
And broken glass dull and out of the sea's reach.

Against hard tidal winds, sand hisses
Racing for the lee of what's lying exposed,
Not yet buried, their grainy shadows
Reaching beyond the wave-toss.

The beach with high tide's edges posted,
The rusted signs of lonely warnings that go unheeded,
Unable to turn back the sea's dissolving into sky,
Loosening the horizon, read:

Beach Logs Kill

and all around in the pattern of tossed pick-up-sticks

for another gamey day, chain-sawed timber

the diameter of garage doors, the length of jets;

Beware of Mountain Lion Attacks

with little to be done but stroll a hungry universe,

barefoot between dislodged barnacles, scuttling crabs,

and the swooping gulls feeding along the shimmer;

Ocean Makes the Rules,

As if it'd been forgotten that *Eternity is not measured*

in duration, as she wades ankle deep

in the salt spray sweeping the shore.

Coastal Rain

She stands beside a wooden picnic table.
The shelter roof in Cosmos Park leaks

Through constellations of bullet-sized holes.
Rain floods the carved messages of
myriad threats and promises.

The knife is tossed from this leaky shelter
and sinks into a mown field.

Stranded, she times the splashes between droplets,
the down-spout ripped off and wrapped

around a support post, freeing the rain to run.

3

Today is fair. Tomorrow it may be overcast with clouds.

—Chief Seattle

High Wires

1 Parental Advice

We can't get around that
    set of plans.
It doesn't mean that we follow
    the straight-and-narrow,
that we plan anything at all,
    or that we fall into someone else's plan,
maybe not meant for us,
    or meant for us and still we let it happen.
We perceive a plan in order to devise
    another plan. We stumble
between plans and act as if we don't care.
    Rarely is not caring the case.
In ancient Antioch the citizens belonged
    to both synagogue and church,
hedging their bets that the Romans
    wouldn't slay both at the same time.
They coughed dust either way—
    confident of the plan.

.

❖

Morning traffic, eight lanes

looping the city, has stopped.

Even at this early hour,

even leaving earlier than needed.

A mother turns to see her son,

half asleep in the seat,

his head against

the closed window, rocking slightly

with each lurch forward.

Northbound between Olive and Page,

trucks and cars another layer

of concrete. Who could conceive

of such potential, idling beyond

possibility: obstruction, construction,

asleep-at-the-wheel,

engine fire, fatalities? They will never know.

Both her hands grip the steering wheel,

she turns again to her half-awake son,

"This is another reason. If you were married,

you'd be taking a cab."

2 Altitude Sickness

The cloudy paradox half-erased in speed,
in exhaustion, the terminal wait,
the wolf's hour, the witch's hour,
another damned hour.

We memorize theorems,
axioms, formulas, equations
that never knew a number.

Something will work out
if worked long enough.

Enough hope, error, mistake,
leads us to seven miles above earth's
dismantling rain forest
and exurban sprawl.

Passengers and patients marvel
through scratched
triple-paned portholes.

The etheric realms
the final resting place

of rhombohedrum
and isosceles triangle.

Fissioned clouds wind-shifted,
thermal-shaped, light-quilted,
dissolving Pythagoras, Plato,
Picasso. God perfecting perfection.

Jet-streamed transhuman
wandering: will we ever
end not wanting.

3 Flight Plan

To the small child who won't stop crying
in the middle of a three hour flight,
two rows back and across the aisle,
not that you can hear this over your own
raging anguish, but I want you to know,
though that probably won't ever happen,
that I'm all with you, and I'm ready to join in
though there's probably an undercover
sky marshal ready to jump into action
if an adult joins in the hysterics,
a privilege only allowed the newly arrived,
though we are all departed here, even though
this child doesn't know it's flailing feet
are 6 miles above the earth,
buckled into a metal tube, propelled by
an enormous noise greater than itself,
that's helping to explode a larger hole
in the atmosphere, and not even the Mickey
and Minnie Mouse cumulus clouds can offer any kind
of calming vision, and even when you scream "daddy"
and your voice cracks and the air
splinters and the wings of the plane
begin flapping, a pterodactyl having swallowed

something unintended and now is frantically

trying to escape what's inside it, the register

of this wailing rising until a spasm of coughing

exhausts the whole endeavor, and passengers realize

in the sputtering silence that we are all lone survivors

of what we have loved in this moment until

the blue smoke of the plane's tires scorch the runway.

4 Round Trip

Breathless beatitude this altitude,
a touch of vertigo above visions
of cirrus and cumulus. The metal wing
an acute angle with the horizon, a triangulation,
its center an aquamarine afterglow.
Another world, longing for tales
of those who return alien and astonished.

My father's fluid-choked lungs succumb
for a third time this day to what his body
can no longer resist, a sinking flight
beyond a hospital bed. From the fourth story
window, reading another chapter to the tops of trees
feathering evening light across the highway,
above bloody bracelets of braking rush hour traffic,
the hurry and wait, the weight we carry
up steep slopes of darkening five o'clock skies.
The nurse waits, wanting to know.

I bend over his shriveled body that hasn't responded
in days, and more slowly than a distant plane
plummeting seven miles back to earth,
he moved his head once up and down.

The nurse left the room as I held his hand,

and after the final release, his hand back at his side,

I turned away and was again looking down at Wyo-

ming, at Idaho, at Washington,

perched on the edge of night.

5 Staying with Friends

My small wood-paneled corner
of steeply sloped sky—I'm learning
to sleep in the attic. All the constellations
and newly minted novas have runoff
down the gutter. Liminal hints
descant in swirls of the downspout.

The mattress is shelved among books.
It's morning. My spine broken open.
Sparrows and pigeons spill out.
Beaks to lips, twitter to thick tongue,
sing together. Rafters my pinions,
roof hips and valleys my folded wings.
Ridge sitter, I flock with the others,
ready to plummet to the backyard feeder.

Webbed all night in treetops,
telephone and electric lines,
a steady hum of stars
and their transcendent transmissions.

Dormer dosing undisturbed
by the busy street,
only to awaken to the occult
hungers of galactic birds.

Day After the Election

Beauty, carburetor, sheepshank, pagoda, absence, chalk,
vector, Amarillo, garters, dromedary, Tartarus, tupelo,
omelet, caboose, ferrocyanide and so on.

—Richard Wilbur

Too late for Beauty, so a beauty withheld

becomes hope adrift.

Beauty with a bloody knife.

Beauty with rifle scope crosshairs and no rifle.

The Beauty of bold headlines.

Persistent Beauty like the shadows on walls

and bridges impressed by a Hiroshima heat.

Beauty no longer caught

in the act of forever is forever.

Beauty in the crushed lizard

under wheels of a prospecting Utah oil thumper.

Beauty in cleaning out the throat of day's carburetor,

all days with a built-in obsolescence.

Beauty in the dull progress of light sans fuel injection.

Night sky a mechanical glitter,

a sheepshank drawing us tighter,

a knotted pagoda choking with a chalky absence.

What vector do we follow through Amarillo,

passing high-finned Cadillacs diving

into hard-pan panhandle plains–

silk panties and garters still scattered across

the pack-rat eaten leather seats. Better

an elected fool on a swift dromedary
headed for Tartuarus than Tupelo.
Let slaverous officials eat cold omelets.
Leave no caboose behind swinging
signal lanterns and going nowhere.
Headlighted Beauty drawing up the rear
in the open convertible, honking
and pointing at a Prussian blue sky,
shouting *Ferrocyanide for president.*

Cannibal Rain

The back window of the car leaks, shattered
in a robbery to steal something not worth
stealing, and the new glass never sealed
watertight. Unlike the terrarium, where
inside its clear walls a hand-sized lizard

is shedding its skin, it's sealed, and there
will never be a rain of lizards in this room.
Thunder, an inch and a half of rain
in half-an-hour, and it's not half done.
The calendar, four months late in finding

a wall, lies on the back car seat. The fountain
in front of the Nymphenburg Palace is wet,
wrinkled, over-flowing in two dimensions.
If a black vinyl seat could cry, that's what it's
doing, as droplets drip from the window and run

down its smooth, cold face across a collection
of too easily pictured days. The lizard's skin has
torn free of its chest and is flung open, a jacket
caught in a wicked wind. Lapels of dry blue
translucent scales take wing. But a ghost of

itself stills clings in rags to its back; two rippled

ribbons split by its brown spine. A papery self

that no longer fits. The gutters are a metronome

of runoff. A steady down-turned bucket-beat

enters through the walls and windows.

The creek rushes to empty itself with a raised hind leg.

The lizard claws off the final shreds and stuffs

its mouth with old skin. Covered with a plastic sheet,

the window still leaks. One of us wants to sit in the

back and dissolve into the Nymphenburg fountain.

Treading Water

1 Trolling

As if he could write the sea
and not spill a drop.
The sea erases it all without help.
Wave-tossed inattentions:

gull feathers, cracked crab shells,
quartz-veined stones, withered kelp
bladders, sinews and shoulders of driftwood.
Now and then he turns to face

the broken white-lipped slur
of insucking water, the white froth,
the pebble rattle, the abacus click
of mineral against mineral,

the steady calculations of a beach.
At tide line a zebra-striped beetle—
wings that won't close
except to be broken,

that won't fly but fly apart,
too delicate to keep.

Something spouts a plume
of water far beyond his certainty.

Silver-pontooned seaplane flies
even farther out into the encircling sea.
Closer the quick jab of gulls,
the race of sandpipers typing

clawed stories into wet sand:
read quickly and revise, read and quickly erase.
Mist-shrouded shorelines.
Islands float out to sea. Shadowless

light. Gray hull on grayer water,
a cargo ship slips off a horizon.
Spent waves sheet the beach.
He tries hard for the final line.

2 Climatic Tides

Voices travel over the rolling water.

The waves shout too.

One says, "Come get me."

The other answers, "I'm coming."

The first says, "Are you sure you want to do this?"

The water so wide it sinks below itself.

Ebb tide: here's eight feet of kelp and barnacled

rock exposed around the cove. Where could it

have gone? All the water that will ever be

on earth, in all our bodies and faucets,

was here from all the beginnings

that only end in each one of us .

The rotting teeth of sea-stacks take bites

out of the waves. An old man, out early

after last night's storm, combs the beach sand.

He holds up a fossilized shrimp, an amber

translucence and in the center a cavity

half-filled with water like a carpenter's level

from an ancient sea that is the mother

of this sea that seethes and rises to new levels.

3 Deception Pass

Whatever excuse: bum knee, six hours late, accidental
meeting in a parking lot two thousand miles from
home, the welling ocean, a surge of threatening desires.

The details, stuck pins in a wall, the plaster around
each hole cracking and peeling into a dangerous,
forbidden geography of channels and straits.

It's where we swim each day, risking riptides,
undertows of a three dimensional world as we pray
to make sense of it all. It's in the anchor of each finger

grasping at treacherous currents, our tremulous lives
swept past without water wings, life jackets,
buoy-roped perimeter, every other galactic shore

eluding us. What's pinched between two islands
that almost touch and never will, except below
the storm-wracked tide line. For the weak

and faint of heart, the arched bridge span
joins rock and road, Fildalgo and Whidbey Islands,
trestled finger above the spinning fir and pine

growing toward a downward summing that accounts

for the shearing water, the delight of crossing

salty turbulence—dead and alive, we float for awhile.

4 Dog Beach

Clammers on the sand of success,
carry their buckets back from tidal flats.

Their three-pronged tridents hooked
on swaying, swinging handles.

The afternoon parking lot unusually crowded
with small-time Neptunes.

5 Portage Bay

Hidden in the yellow primrose that crowds

under the shock of weeping willow branches,

it's easy to see sadness in its breezy shrug

sweeping across the surrounding lavender,

as if grief must be made sweet as it drags

us down into water's folding reflections.

I'm listening to the small monotonous stories

that the waves tell lapping the channel's

concrete walls. Their wet lips tired,

discarded by boat wakes,

kissing again and again

the smooth hulls of the rich.

Against the posted warnings of feeding: disease,

dependence, over-population, I break a granola bar

into pieces for the ducks that dodge

Everything Negotiable, The Money Shot, Seadation,

boats passing boats. The pigeons waddle

and peck around the bench and bushes.

High-masted pleasure boats conspire

to raise the bridges of the poor, believing

their place is to be first to the other side,

as stopped traffic idles then continues

its shuffle along the boulevard

and fanciful U-turns onto 520 West.

Mare Tranquillitatis

I made it to the moon and nothing changed.
If I had something urgent to say nothing changed.
If I made it beyond the moon, lost in so much distance,
Space out of space out of space, nothing changed.
Perhaps a fiercer loneliness.

If I didn't have something urgent to say nothing
Changed. Not the daily or weekly drive to the grocery
Store. At the mall, just to remain a target,
A moving target to stay in the game.

You on that other coast, that far side of the moon,
That none of us, caught on this paltry side
In this fusion of light and shattered star glitter,
Can see and imagine and almost always get it wrong.

Midnight, blood silver and cold.
The needle a possum crawling under your skin.
Still a need to say the something of nothing.
The odometer has turned insane, the body is rusting
Out, and I could be talking about a car.

To drive, no driven. I always thought
The stratosphere was the limit. Now I know,
Shedding the scales of gravity, coins taped
Over my eyes, I lift off to walk on the moon.

You Are the Most Eatable

"You have to be careful what you fall in love with in your twenties. I fell in love with this island."

—George Divoky, Avian Researcher,
Cooper Island, Alaska

Holtz Bay to the west, Chichagof Point to the south.
Always carry a shotgun and a walkie-talkie,
if there's anyone else on the island or not. No wife,
no lover in decades, friends far between, only the daily
churlish hello and goodbye of frigid waves.

An occasional and not so occasional starving polar bear
swims to the island as Arctic ice retreats farther
to the north and the permafrost is no longer permanent.
Thirty thousand years of ancient village sites
exposed and eroding, the frozen bodies

climb out of embankments, rotting for the first
and last time. Not here, there's only a single cabin
on the highest low spot though who knows what's un-
derneath the sand and gravel. The ceaseless clatter of
surf and the rolling roulette of steel-gray pebbles

keep adding up and endlessly subtracting until sea lev-
el rise sinks the island. Then finally the issue laid
to rest or submerged. He's spent forty-three summers
observing and counting the Black Guillemots, their rise
and now their fall. Their food, a small cod disappears

with the edge ice. The roundtrip flights too far, their
chicks starve when not devoured by bears.
He tears open a dead chick lying on the gravel,
stomach empty. No leaving this island alive,
as he stares off into icy light of a summer setless sun.

Cargo Cult

1 Flights

Morning pigeons brake, flutter,
land just above the gutter
outside the dormer window.

Squeeze themselves down into the alley.
So much weight plummets too fast to stop.
Barely adequate wings beat the air senseless.

The invisible too weak to keep them aloft.
Pinion-flooded cars: keys turn
and turn, batteries run down,

engines sputter, fly wheels heave slowly
to a stop, pistons perch and seize, sparkless.
Rolling off the roof, feathered cars crash

on the grass in heaps, where pigeons
traffic with sparrows
for seeds fallen from the feeder.

2 Wild Woman

On the front porch there are Jean Davis' lilacs
in a clay pot followed by a succession
of pots of various shapes and sizes,
plastic and clay, lined along the bottom
of the iron railing, each one containing
a more desiccated lilac,
the anatomical stages of a losing life.

To one side of the first step off the porch
the burden of an island beach,
an oval white stone laced with black streaks,
scrawl of lightning-strike motions,
disordered emotions, the panic rolling in
an undertow, all there on a pedestal
of chain-sawed, surf-lathed driftwood.

In the sun room, there is no room to sit.
Gangly cactus reach to the ceiling.
To see the backyard from the kitchen
window, leaves must be parted, just to see
more potted plants crowding the bricked patio.

3 Chicken Littlest

A rain of angels or angels of rain?
Is it heaven rising or the sky falling?
Puddles of the forgotten
clog the streets' run-off drains.

Rain scratches the windows—
half-horror film, half cat wanting in.
This room unnaturally cold. The rescued
couch rocks in others' wakes.

The gutters are choking, forced
to swallow every pinioned drop.
It's mass murder all over town
and all the headlines read *Flood*.

Supplicants, funereal dripping hemlock boughs.
Keep-on-rowing gushes from downspouts
over spongy lawns. No one listens.
Raincoats transcend lives.

Fear always obliging.

The forecast dire.

Sidewalks the stinking canals of Venice.

Umbrellaed pedestrians walk on water.

.

4 Apartment Time

The heater's metallic tick,

an arrhythmic beat:

expansion/contraction,

diastole/systole,

load the gun/unload the gun,

and other erratic exuberances

of failed time.

We demand the gear-meshed measure,

the steady battery beat,

wall-clock exactness,

the obedient wrist-watch wait.

The short tree by the window

is decorated with cookie-cutter ornaments.

Green wallet of poverty's holiday countdown.

The potted plant by the door—

shoe-sized with ship-shaped leaves—

pulled from a dumpster,

harbors its own thirsty clock.

Waist-high stacked books across the floor:
towers of Babel, steepled knowledge,
precarious spires, tumbling heavenward,
leaning into locked rooms.

5 Forgotten History

He gave his daughter a book of poems
for her birthday. She decides
it's not for her and hands the book
back to him, a document too hermetic to
bother to decode. He places it on
a high shelf. Years later, visiting, she is
lying under a blanket on the couch.
He sits in a chair across the room
under lamplight. The windows are
stroked with night. He reads the first
two poems from the book. She listens
as his voice drifts through the dark
and settles into the chair. She says that's
the book he stole from her.

Art of Tools

—Tacoma, Washington

At the Museum of Glass, there's not a single vial
blown to collect the tears of Caesar or hold
the desert fragrances of Pharaonic dynasties.
No splintered shards of Krystallnacht
scattered across the floor,
or Liberace's chandelier that hung
over flaunting piano recitals
as America pondered its own gay music.

Amid the phalanx of guards holding visitors
at arm's length, works hang or are pedestaled,
worn down to glistening under patron's eyes.
No Mozart symphony piped in to ease
the worked-over brittle heart. There's
an over-sized glass hammer about to strike
an over-sized glass nail so we can see through
the unmaking; a stone loaf smoothly sliced

by a rice paper blade in this version of the weak
overcoming the meek; a school of vise grips welded
into one fishy direction, a metal ton schooling
against the net of one wall; a century-old six-foot

cross cut saw, each two-inch wide tooth wrapped tight

as a mummy, the pink taffeta disarming,

as if trying to save the northern rainforest

from the ravenous 19th century.

The Untamed

—Chief Leschi School

Hula hoop harnessed around the waist
to pull anyone in clinging to the circumference.

Yellow balls kicked into unreasoned arcs
randomly punctuate the air.

Climb the ladder and climb more. Climb out
of sight, slide down from the low gray clouds.

Jump from the wooden platform
and leave two prints deep in muddy earth.

From the nearby slough, a flock of ducks
scatter before an eagle.

Slip down the pole. Throw the ball
through the hoop. Up the tube tunnel not down.

The daily challenge
how high can the swing go?

Crawl along the ground.

Roll over the gravel.

Run like you can't be stopped,

Don't ever tire.

Across the field the train clatters on.

The Puyallup River carries Rainier's whiteout

with the squeals, the screams, the cries.

Holy Victrola Café

Copy machine run wild, self-replicating

cubicle dream that threatens the inside horizon.

A stutter that never reaches its word.

At each table someone is bent over a journal

typing at a laptop: dark details of Vermeer,

the stepping-off-the-edge of Magritte.

A few write backwards, revising their lives,

inking out blurred visions early on a summer

Sunday morning. Cup balanced in one hand,

she carries a wobbly wooden chair

out to the curb and faces Charles' Produce truck

with its painted rainbow cornucopia of vegetables

tumbling across its metal side panel.

It can't squeeze into the space to parallel

park and drives on. Her cotton dress, vined

with black leaves, accented with raspberry-tinted

flowers — she is stunned into bloom. She carefully

lifts the petals of her dress to draw it halfway up

her thighs. Skin glows in the light. A delicate blue-

veined topography maps the slope of muscles

that lead to slashing red toenails strapped into sandals.

Her feet point inward to bring her knees together

to hold up the magazine she's reading. Light wraps

her calves. A solitary pigeon bobs through the scuffed

forest of chair legs. Her latte languishes between

Sue's Natural Remedies and Super Cleaner's

sun-dulled claim of expert alterations.

Rain of Directions

I've been running for years between the vertical
and horizontal rain. Rain that falls like dirt raising un-
told siblings of dust. Rain welded to windows
that smear dry faces that deny their haunting.

Don't ask if I stayed dry or whether my shirt,
soaked, sticks to my chest, nipples
poking through the chill.

There hasn't been much chance to practice lately.
Late summer drought that won't let go
until the grass is strangled to a crisp brown.

An old man sits on a bus bench waiting for what
doesn't come. No choking diesel cloud, no gear-
grinding thunder, no dancing over boxy transformers
and chimneys. The street bone dry of directions.

The dark is under his scalp. Inside his skull
An echo that won't stop, an itch in the blood.
It's all that's still wet. And that's how he leaves it.

A gash, an alluvial flow over the sidewalk.

He's drying up from the inside out.

The culmination of every argument.

No one left standing. A run through the rain.

I hit the ground before the droplets

and miss the liquor store shoot out.

A neon open sign flashes holes in the night.

Interruption at the End

—for Ken Shepard

I haven't seen the end
or if I did see the end
I didn't know. The litany
of denials, the most blindingly likely,

and now I spend too much time
thinking about the end,
conspiring to pretend
to say something of the end,

and then a piece of the end
arrives instantly intact from
half-a-continent away—
a phone call, a jogging trail

beside a creek that went awry
in hundred degree heat,
a trail with a new end
as old as any and all of us.

Speechless

—for Alan

The Olympics soften.
Across the chilled sound,
ridges dissolve to pale blue seams

outlined by stars.
All around the city buildings are lost.
The downcast cones of streetlights

catch the corner of a supermarket,
the front of a dusty used bookstore,
a Mongolian barbecue. Tangled

in luminous shrouds of light, the mangled
neon of Bimbo's, the Green Cat Café,
the Coffee Messiah, all warning of a life.

Down steep steps to 2nd Avenue NW,
the western red cedar that blocked the view,
that made the descent secretive,

folding quietly into its heavy green fronds,
was felled to clear out the sewer line.
The driest July on record scatters

the scent of lavender. There is always
so much to say, to say again, to calm,
to reassure, to hold back a moment

more. Edgar, the neighborhood tabby
strolls up, fed and pampered at three houses,
purrs around any ankle. Released

from the day's heat, the car
on a darkening street waits
to remember to drive away.

4

Tribe follows tribe, and nation follows nation,
like the waves of the sea.

—Chief Seattle

Until Next Time

Nothing can fully wake us
except the next thrust
of pain. All of us tired,
faces pudgy with disbelief
and lack of sleep.
So little we can do

for protection, except hide
some sane fragment
of self, hoping it survives
and can be recalled,
and is not so deeply disguised
that once the slipping begins

there's nothing left to recall us.
We sit, heads bowed, sinking
to our knees, meaty balloons
losing their helium. This is the party
we joined and want to abandon.
One of us mentions the pack mule

dragged off last night
by a jaguar. Another, the horse
a snake killed before noon.
We never saw it, only heard
the screaming whinny and collapse.
After ascending the high pass,

a second horse broke through ice
crossing an unnamed river.
At least here, where we have fallen
in the snow, into our exhaustion,
there aren't insects giving us
a shadow more loyal than the one

that follows us the rest of our questionable
days. Maybe the stomach parasites
that doubled us over will abandon
us to wander lower altitudes. Growing cold,
we feel the botfly maggots shivering
in the burrows of our skin.

We didn't stumble quickly enough
through the mud and undergrowth
so our hands and feet are covered
with a glowing fungus. We submerge

them in the icy water until fingers
and toes turn blue. No powdery-winged

moths to burn our eyes. No bats to piss
in our faces as we sleep. No leaves
covered with toxins. No flesh-eating
protozoans requiring weeks of intravenous
antimony till we return to the future
of our pasts. No roving gangs

of irate hungry peccary.
Staring at our coffee cups, this is what
we worry over at the S & M Café in Cairo, MO.
We recall Uncle Joe, after he went missing
for two days, relatives and neighbors
thinking he'd gone to town and stayed

with a new octogenarian girlfriend
or too drunk to drive, until his eye glasses
and false teeth were found smashed
in the mud of the hog pen, and that was it.
It's worry that gives us a body
to survive the day.

By Now

Stars scorch the charred dome of heaven.

Blackened windows stare in and out.

Cats fed too early wander the house.

The suitcase sat on, latched, sits by the door.

Coffee cup emptied a second time.

Last minute hesitations folded into a pocket.

How far we travel to never arrive.

Backing up, caught in the sweep of headlights:

sawhorses, ladder, basketball hoop,

a yard comfortable in its chaotic shadows.

The field blinded, stunned naked with light.

Thick fog curls from night's lips.

In a few hours, sun will candle the tops of oaks.

He will awaken twice from the same night's bed.

Almost there, she must have turned off the highway.

What leaves left turn red and purple into their own fall.

Cold clamped to the skin of a second startled departing. Tickets, like leaves blow across the counter.

Ruins of breakfast to be cleared from the table.

Surely, by now, she's through security and into

the insecure world.

Parisian Back Pains

She backed in, didn't look,
didn't know she needed to look
backing down on her back
in the living room. Feet flat on the floor,
knees raised, triangulated flesh and bone,
twin Eiffel Towers. Buttocks pressed plainly,
ungainly against the floor.

No tourists to crowd the walk ways,
to hug the railings, to pinion
alien fantasies of flying into a harmless world.
No centuries-stained, tile roof-ridge perches,
no gilt-framed vertigo before spiraling down
into her thousands-of-miles away back pain.

Backed down to an exotic bug-eyed level
with the rug: abandoned ant trails
ending in a poisoned reward, cockroaches
and spiders making mad dashes to the next
shadow, too often a black widow,
once the upcurled tail of a scorpion.

All to ease her back, knees to chest
working toward a fetal optimism,
wanting to stand up for any cause,
desperate to declare bipedalism a success,
storm the brachiating primate barricades,
still she's backed against the rug.

Backward, she wriggles and squirms,
makes fine adjustments, a spine
corseted in canvas and steel blades wraps
her torso, cinched with Velcro and lace.
She sits Eiffel Tower straight.

What next? To watch her stand,
pressing slowly up from the floor,
first with her elbows, then grabbing
the chair seat, leveraging the arm rest,
gripping the table's edge,
these the contortions, distortions,
to climb the barricade of Parisian pain.

Indigo Empire

Already mascaraed rivers of grief.
Already a fidgeting silence blackens the hall.

Tongueless howls, savage claims.
We know the umpire's blind when we're losing

and we always are. It doesn't matter, strikes, balls,
stealing home, the ball knocked out of the catcher's

well-worn mitt after the runner's body-block diving for
home—no officiating as the ball rolls into the dugout.

Maybe I settled into "officiate" when there was no
turning back for third base, home ahead,

and for this woman who sat up in bed at 4 a.m.,
saying she couldn't sleep, who was so happy,

if not giddy, during the dinner party, but this hour be-
fore mocking bird and cardinal announce

themselves in the first skeins of light, in her studio
she holds a gallon of indigo over her head, and dyed

her body. She became a shadow of her shadow,
her nipples surging fonts of darkness,

pubis dripping a dark mystery, hips'
outriggers sailing into a fathomless sea,

thighs trellised with streaks,
feet following the irrevocable flow

in an already smothering summer heat.
With stepladder and rope she evaded

the coming hours, no longer hiding yet hidden,
shielded, protected in her indigo gown. Someone

I didn't know, only our common recognizable
namelessness, but not today, not that we know

what we never thought, yet already after the words,
the songs, the poems, the fiddle's case

snapped closed, the officiating finished,
the evening sky tightens into indigo.

Postcard from Venice

If I had known that for her
it must always be famous:
the sky sapphire, the horizon

snowcapped mountains,
the slopes folding and flowering
in a rich effacing purple,

the shallow sea spreading
undisturbed below her window,
except for an excursion boat

that dissolves in its own wake
as it maneuvers toward
a sea-stained dock.

Purled reflections of arched
pavilions. Centuries before
thieves, and those out of favor,

entered the sea wall's small room
at low tide, hands tied, door locked,
waiting for the condemned

water to rise. The moon's flight
could save them, but didn't.
Whatever else she mentions:

wild boar and saddle of venison
in Vienna, baby octopus in a quiet village
on the island of Burano,

the glacé of Florence, all this
a kind of reprieve from
her day to day drowning.

Natural Causes

Is it the freshly raked dirt and sand of the *corrida*?
Not a foot or hoof print visible. The audience here
to cheer a Zen rock garden? The band plays
the *pasodoble* in the brassy evening sun of seven o'clock.
The trumpet defiant, brave, lonely, exalts.
The arena swollen with long shadows.
Light hovers over the flagged stadium rim.
Certain of death in the *plaza de toros*,
The picador high on his horse drives the lance.
The thick-roped muscles begin to unwind.
What good a charging bull, if its head is not down,
horns pointed at a tossed salvation?
The bull's neck further coifed with gaily colored
banderillos to complement the blood.
The matador steps forward following the flourishes
of his cape. He is calm as a rose in a vase.
The bull charges and meets the sword.
The snorting half ton becomes a carcass.
If the bull is the gallant one, the crowd cheers
for the bull. If the matador is fearless,
the dead bull loses its ears, the bloody shells paraded
around the ring to hear the crowd's ringing adulation.

Prague Floods, 2002

...the Germans will think the Czechs use strange chairs.

— Antonin Strizek

The Vltava River must be tired
leaning back in an oversized chair
kicking its soggy feet
over the bank,
taking a break,
smoking a misty cigarette,
sipping latte-colored currents
swirling along abandoned streets,
humans the only measure to measure
twisting around bridge pilings.

Time to move on to the next job
in the next city with more furniture
to float off, making the rounds
through living rooms and kitchens,
couches and beds to rearrange,
a sodden interior redesigner—
this river's exuberant
late summer decor.

In the municipal library,

the river reads too easily

the proclamations, the declarations

of ousted communists and party hacks.

On its way to North Sea beaches,

it drops the news

of counter revolutions

and aging reactionaries.

Old manifestoes compost

with cabbage leaves

in German backyards.

Water music is heard

slipping through the Mala Strana.

When the wet score recedes

twenty-three grand pianos

are tuned to silt and followed

by a concerto

of crowbars and hammers.

How water loves to act

at the Archa Theater:

submerged avant-garde performances

punctuated by a stutter of bubbles,

as if the secret police

were still decoding each new wave.

The Old Jewish Cemetery
with its decks of stacked headstones
waits to be reshuffled and dealt
again the same losing hand.
Treading water the croupier
is washed away.

Magdelena Jelelove's oversized chair
with the river seated comfortably
in the contemporary art museum courtyard,
is destined for a garden in Leipzig,
confirming the Czech's broad-seated oddity.

Apocalyptic Exhaustion

1

Only rock-hard people know stone thoughts.
More chipped, fissured, fractured,

but always a throw away from escape.
Stones the only thinking creatures in this bleak tundra.

Better to be buried in moss and lichen behind walls
of wire below watchtowers.

Maybe the stones possess freedom, unevenly set
in mortar and stacked to block others.

Women inmates underfed, jacketless in subzero
        weather,
in rooms barely heated, hunt mice and call it a five-star
        meal.

Diagnosed with collective mass psychosis, they talk in
        tongues
that belong to no tribe of the snow-blind.

They walk through walls believing in transcendence.
Wild-eyed, their hair electrical storms, they dance

for hours before collapsing into the arms of a dire
calendar.

2

Rubles back in circulation, winter savings to be spent
in small towns east of the capital, but the shelves
are stripped bare. The grocer wonders about
another order for matches, kerosene, sugar, candles.

The big day, days away, and if he's still around,
he could place a new order, and if he doesn't
quick profits will be lost.

After the end, he wonders what his customers plan
with all they've hoarded. Will they return to a place lit
only by fire, a dim flickering light to shape to an unre-
lenting dark? Will hunger become a savage god?

Is there another end after the end? He's decides it isn't
worth the effort, he'd be overstocked with inventory af-
ter the end.

3

Who can tell the difference: the government claims

secret *methods of monitoring planetary changes,*

and with absolute certitude concludes

nothing out of the usual for December 21, 2012,

though the citizenry will still be vulnerable to the usu-

al: *blizzards, ice storms, tornadoes, floods,*

trouble with transportation and food supply, breakdowns

and always shortages of heat, electricity, and water supply.

Assurances, reassurances, flow like frozen water

from the Chief Sanitary Doctor, the Orthodox Church,

the Duma, and a former disc jockey,

who recently placed first in the television show,

"Battle of the Psychics."

Starting on December 22nd, it's illegal

to spread news of the apocalypse. The halls of justice

already overflow to the end and after.

4

Perhaps it's government policy that no one should sur-
vive. It's easier to govern that way.

The church has assured the shaky that *doomsday is sure
to come*, but not by coming up short on an ancient
long-count calendar and *so-called parade of planets*,
but from moral decline.

In Prison Colony No. 10 inmates escape
into endless drifts of snow, return blue
disturbed by the swirling vortex of their thoughts.
Seizures and panic attacks are daily, hourly.

An inmate in morning formation declares the earth
just yawned and the others run in all directions
until Revelation is read by Reverend Tikhon Irshenko
revealing the true end.

In Ulan-Ude and the factory town of Omutninsk,
food is hoarded, candles are gone. Nothing to fuel
the last supper not even the dark.

The shopkeeper's made enough money to spend the holidays farther south on warmer ice.

Statues

Robed men stare at the undulating heat
of horizons and are driven mad.

Eyes scorched, they drive over the edge
of small clusters of clay-brick houses.

A few goats wonder a bare hillside,
a dog cowers behind an earthen oven,

the small plots of irrigated barley are
bleached bandages over parched fields.

Along dirt roads, they wave Kalashnikovs
in greeting. Through Bamiyan their trucks

trail long wakes of boiling dust. Hood-
mounted flags beat down the dirty air.

Imaginations less than perfect,
no image of God good enough.

They arrive with antiaircraft guns.
Not even a God really

just a man who once understood
the root of suffering. Not even a man now

but the avalanche of sandstone slabs.
Hands explode.

A Toyota-sized toe protrudes from the rubble.
A Buddha alive.

Red-muzzled fingers rip at sandstone.
Giant stone fingers severed in welcome.

Not even a God really, but a man
who saw through suffering,

saw a world suffering us.
Slabs of chest shake the ground.

Face detonated into ten thousand
faces. Armless, legless.

They missed the everlasting stone.
They missed the stone.

Bye Bye Olduvai

You are so far south I keep
looking down at my thumb.
Written on the wrinkled skin
just below the joint
the neon blue veins fan out
flashing the name Utopia.

It's easy to be distracted
by billboards for yet
another upscale, out-of-town
subdivision. Dressed in
suits of nails and wearing
panama hats, their thumbs live

curled in mansions below
pink palms. Even
in this unsellable story
death is grasped, but thinks it's
so far off and south
it would take an extra lifetime

so I don't have time
to reconsider. Instead its door

will come knocking.

In the book I'm thumbing through,

I skip a couple of pages

to the longing of birds

in cages and lesser

avian desires. She wants

her hair cut so it will be

alive as peacock feathers

swaying in the draft

from the air duct.

My hair is a highway

of coiffed thumbs. Naturally,

their bones begin to lose

their grip and hitch for

the floor just when I need

a new destination. We could be

hairless and happy in Utopia

but thumb screws are tightened,

as dictated. Index fingers

point and squeeze. Hair

on the back of knuckles grows

quietly dangerous suburbs.

Photographing the Wind

All photographs are accurate
None of them is truth.

—Richard Avedon

The bird in the photograph has already

Abandoned the air and stands

On barren ground, a lord with folded

Wings, statuesque, a feathered black

Granite that has dropped from an African

Sky. Though the bird looms large

And too alert, it's in the background,

And on this all too clear and sunny day

We know the bird can't be blamed.

This is simply what it knows best.

Though it may have arrived a little

Early, it is certain in its waiting.

The naked child, has drawn her knees

Up to her chest, her forehead pressed

Against years of parched ground,

Her forearms stretched forward

And away from either side

Of her bone-thin body, her back

To the steadfast bird, guardian
Of this warring, drought-stricken plain.

This is when we want to believe in a wind
Such as this one crossing the porch
And cooling our cups of coffee,
That refuses to carry a cry or spread
The scent of finality, and instead braids
Strands of warmth through the cool
Evening, between the spaces of
Our outspread fingers, our hands failed
Kites, our lives falling through this luxurious air.

Transformational Grammars

In Lingala, a slow river lexicon,

                a dense jungle syntax,

a parrot squawk punctuation, an antelope tone.

                Deep in the dripping

leaves syllabic shadows — yesterday

                tomorrow, mired in today.

Epidemics of equatorial heat

                disease each day. Night festers

in a deafening screech and wail. In the floral-print

                shirt lying on a dirt floor,

a mildewed anguish grows. Once Congo, then

                Zaire, Congo again transforms

colonial decay into uprooted rain forest.

A cup breaks in the sink,

                handle snapped off.

For a few hours it sits on

                the counter waiting to be glued,

but then is thrown out. I hear the painted

                tropical butterflies, iridescent

against a glazed white background, flutter against

the trash can lid-wing beats over a

river of refuse. Tomorrow and yesterday breaking

down into today.

Hex Hunt

—Uganda

What does it take to be a *witch*?

What does it take to accuse a witch

of being a witch and not just some

coffee-maker-broke morning that throws

someone into a lack-of-caffeine witchiness?

Too many broomsticks in the closet?

Candles burning in circles? A scattering

of unidentified bones that the dog might have

dragged into the yard? Plastic skull flowerpots

on the porch railing? Walking in the wrong direction,

maybe backwards, and not just lost? Coughing up

phlegm with a face floating in the shivering gelatinous

mass? Limping as if two people were walking

in one body? Killing a chicken after dark?

Humming an enchanting tune that others can't forget?

Strangers flying through a bedroom? Neighbors

who talk only when standing on their heads?

And what exactly does it take to kill a witch:

special weapon, ritual, curse, to insure the witch

stays dead? Mere hanging or stacking stones

on the accused chest to stop breathing?

Drowning and if the body floats then the person

was belatedly innocent? Perhaps burning at the stake

is still standard practice, or hoe and machete enough

in the tropics where heat casts a deathly spell,

humidity the madness of the hexed heart.

Freetown Rain

—Sierra Leone

The city's citizens
                    jittery as leaves
under a rain of bullets.
                    A man calmly walks the middle
of the street
his arms bent at the elbows,
                            his forearms folded
across his chest
        cradling his upturned severed hands
as if begging for rain
                to wash him away.

Angola to Zanzibar

1

Somehow we find ourselves a beginning.
Some days it takes thousands of miles
and someone else to recognize it.
Even then we may pass quickly
from city to city. In one market
dozens of burros crowd around
the only tree in the village,
their tethered heads all facing the trunk.
Like fallen leaves draped over their shoulders,
buyers wrapped in brown robes circle
the gray rumps. In a far corner,
which is only dusty air, a group
of men dressed in suits and ties gather
into their own small knot. No one knows
where they have come from or why they are
here; perhaps to sell another God or hurt
someone. Beyond the beaten earth
of the market, on the edge of the dry savanna,
under a dome of cloud-thatched sky,
in front of all that is ever home,

two sisters smile, eager to tell their story,

but it begins in another language, and for

a few coins they smile broadly for the camera.

2

On a dirt road that barely remembers

a direction, that is really only a memory

of a destination, a teenage boy, his forehead

painted with a white down-turned arc

that echoes his brows and has the grace

of an ancient Etruscan helmet, stops

and rests on crutches, temporarily hobbled

by his rite of circumcision. He accompanies three

young girls, each with a baby. Around their

necks are disk necklaces, flat as rings

of Saturn that stretch beyond their shoulders

and spin off a universe of colors.

One baby balanced on her mother's hip

is blind in the right eye. There are days

on this plain as long and dark and permanent,

but they continue on and out of sight

toward some dusty center.

3

There are pink horizons and flocks
of flamingoes that stretch as far.
Light interrupted only by dust.
There are calderas that circle
erupted worlds. Blood drunk from
the goblets of slashed rib cages.
Elephants tear down block buildings
looking for water; wrench pipes from
walls — plumbers with trunks. The empty
cattle corrals are five-feet-high tangles
of thorned acacia branches, centered on
the herder's dung-plastered hut. These are
the final acts of waiting for the rains.

5

It matters little where we pass the remnant of our people.
They will be few . . . .

— Chief Seattle

Flying Economy

To say nothing is meaningful
is to say everything is what?
One time or another, leaf humus
and clogged drains equally possess our attention.
.

To categorically exclude is to categorically include
what is excluded. One day and another, yo-yoing
between sun up and sun up. Yes, you want it.
No, you don't. It can't be helped.

Maggots crawl around the black plastic bag
draped over the edge of the steel garbage can.
They have nothing to do with this week
or nothing to do until we do, and then everything.

In flint-edged evening light,
the possum flattened on the road.
Rot infects the air. I go to bury it
and scoop its toothy grimace onto a shovel.

There's a perfect white shadow

wriggling in the dust,

a thousand squirming larva

ready for this possum's flight.

Babylonian Moment

I've never so much as now wanted to climb into

the ditch-water- brown metal-walled emptiness

of NR GX 10 14 or even PN JX 51 142

parked on a side rail waiting for the mainline to clear.

The steel-ringed ladder to the top so inviting. It's tradi-

tion to throw one's body into another

hoping to be carried away. Here they sit on rails pol-

ished by mindless traversing, mimicking

the great river only yards away down

the rip-rapped embankment, its glistening surface mo-

tionless in its mile-wide stretch to the other shore.

A steadfast pair, rail and river, the immoveable

moving. The longing of a locomotive calls out

its intentions. The muddy water has its own

wandering white pelican. Highway 61

a few feet farther away slipping with the doppelganger

swish into field and forest. Parallel lives separated

only by troubled strips of grass.

Rail, river, road, the turbulent disorders of civilization,

in the air of Montrose Pioneer Trail Monument Road-

side Park with its parting sign,

Linger Longer. The earth vibrates underfoot and the cars

begin a rusted booming as the black hump-backed coal

cars diesel south. It's not quite quiet

as the pelican glides away, the other cars may

or may not move today, and I can't wait

for another rise and ruin before I leave.

A Mouse of Trouble

Just when you thought the expression of love had
reached its end, run out of gas on some back road
late at night, the only condom in the glove compart-
ment with a hole chewed by a mouse,

and though desire is burning down the house
of your body, the windows melted with the milky
steam of your breath, every muscle shouting
take a chance,

and what's one more chance in this unlucky life that's
always calling ahead with heads when you pick tails,
but this time the coin stands on edge, having fallen be-
tween the seats.

The interior reeks of a mouse that died a month ago
in the ventilation ducts. The cabin filters replaced,
disinfectant and deodorizer sprayed,
its body somewhere between the fan

and the vent controls that can't be turned far enough
from your face, so it goes the slow mummification of
tiny pharaohs and their murdered attendants, and
maybe a wife or two besides,

love floats down this Midwestern Nile air duct, seclud-
ed and safe, but the desire can't overcome
the puddle of fur in the live trap in the trunk,
forgotten as a scorched valentine in summer heat.

Superior Waters

1

Spruce too straight to be anything but telephone poles,
Trucked halfway across a continent,
Wade deep into weeds, poison ivy, sunflowers, keeping
Our voices distant and dry above flooded fields.

2

Clouds stack up as if the wind turned mason,
Pot-bellied and drinking beer to numb
The worn-out cartilage in the machinery
Of its gusty shoulders. The sky's blue mortar
Hardly holds the day together before the sun slips,
Movie-slow, off its scaffolding, to build a darker house.

3

Next to the restaurant's half-burnt out neon sizzle,
A soft gray swirl of sky. Across the highway,
Oil storage tanks sit, metal biscuits on a scraped
Pan of baked earth. Beside the fenced-in satellite dish,
A picnic table with one bench. Underneath August

Crickets begin to count down. A couple strolls

The asphalt parking lot, clockwise, counter-clockwise.

4

Nothing to do once the slapping stops but press myself

Into the warm body of soothing sand and stare

Into the smoky pall where ships' masts sail upward,

Dropping gravity's ballast, before falling toward

A decaying northern port. Out of the rippled blue,

Her arms reach up from the Delft china surface,

A fish leaping into sight, or better into my mouth.

5

Varieties of religious experience so quick and easy,

Said and seen so often meaning, absolutely, resolutely,

Clean, clear. . . and then not so clear, sitting

In the smolder rising from a damp birch log.

In a shroud of flies, I sit shooing them from the lip

Of a coffee cup, the flickering shadows of aspen leaves

Smoking the table covered with rescued beach pebbles,

Cold, weathered hearts of sandstone

As my twelve year-old son tells me to *Get a life*.

6

Wind smooths the wrinkled sheets of smoke.
White-suited birch pack for another season.
So many flies it could be a grim fairytale of black snow
That won't melt. I want to wait for the telling but can't.
The beach is abandoned. A noon mist hurries
Along the shore. Over the blue bound water, light's
scissors cut deep into the waves' telling.

7

Waves stick their tongues in the sand.
A moist shining that the moon licks.
Water polishes the body until it disappears.
Over, through, between: unashamed,
Even as desire pools, floods, is exhausted
Though never quite done with any of us.

Refuse

1   **Tanque Verde**

       —Tucson

Red dune buggy bounces down the wash.
Wide ribbon of corrugated tracks
Tied to the extinction of a fading engine.
Two cherry-helmeted passengers
So lonely here they scream to be heard.

Tall river of a quarter horse ripples past.
Hooves splash sand.
Brown cowboy-hatted rider shouts
At the kids with BB guns not to shoot
Until she's past. The boys turn away
Tired of firing at flocks of cans.

Hunched over in yesterday,
Husband and wife stroll along
With another evening to resolve.
Their daughter and three dogs
Race between boulder-rubbled banks.

He kicks an upright tire half-submerged

In the dry bed—one of a school

Of black-treaded desert dolphins.

It's the start of a long list deposited

For the dry season: broken bricks,

Dented barrels, warped boards,

Ant-infested mattresses, rolls

Of chicken wire, a rusted out car,

All waiting to head south

On this desert avenue, awaiting

the rare compromise of rain.

2   Volcanic Fields

—Albuquerque

Five strands, four points, more straight
Than a crow's flight—barbed wire's impeccable logic
Certain as the horizon that it claims.

Boots press a thin soil delicate as flushed larks.
Stunted yucca bristle and charge the blued air.
Leaves honed on a sharp and fatal light.

Scorched earth swallows the single fruit
Of a half-buried prickly pear. Low clumps
Of brittle grass strewn like shattered glass.

There's the broken box springs of a sleeper
Sailing over the desert, drunk on stars that
Burn out—brief bright scar across the fathomless.

The tangled nerves of tumbleweed struggle to crawl
Under the lowest strand of fence in visions of escape.
Ancient perforated black basalt,

A stone sponge saturated with heat and dying

Stars. Extinct tongue of lava leaves the mesa speechless

With everything lost and everything still to lose.

San Francisco

—Pam McClure

It's ubiquitous and trite, 3 a.m.,
A city that never sleeps only grows
Lonelier: murder, mayhem, malicious pandering,
Larger-than-life spray tags sweeping across
Sidewalks and granite walls, and still the city
Streets are a singular echo of steps following
Sinister echoes. The night undressing as tires
Rip open damp pavement, neon snaking
Along wet curbs, and for the abandoned, time
To cover overstuffed grocery carts with fog.

The sleeper loses his way, physically,
Psychically, sleep walking a matter to be worked
Out later with hotel security. The many complaints:
The jiggled door knobs, the dark glimpsed through
Fish-eyed peepholes, seeing something dragged,
Maybe a body dissolving down the hall,
The way lost, the corridor longer than thought,
Endless, each exit sign pointing to the next door,
And the next, each door hung with *Do Not Disturb*
As the many snore confidentially through their failures.

She listens for a way out, a brush of air, muffled trolley

clang just around the carpeted corner.

The flush of fog beyond the windows,

The blush of neon's electrified air blush,

Whose very sight sets off smoke alarms.

The fire department on the scene: axed and hosed,

laddered to the ninth floor, ready to quell

the suffering that carves out and craves an existence,

lovers in their ruined rooms, the charred promises

that tonight's smoldering will be whole

and freshly curtained with sea fog.

Reno Moon Landing

Fifteen stories and I'm looking for one.
Not a beginning but at the bottom,
where the slots are flashing
a hungry light, day and night devoured.

There are stories that rise higher.
Others hide behind one-way, bronze-
tinted windows, watching the freeway traffic
enter the dark of their own headlights.

We turn our backs and the lights
bubbling up the Sierra foothills go flat,
same as the bottle left uncorked
beside the shrinking, teetering, stack of quarters.

In a neon world, nothing wants to
leave us and our bum luck alone.
Not the woman dressed in bulging spandex,
standing in the next phone booth, shouting,

"I swear. Jesus, I swear," over the jangle of wins

and losses. She pulls me away from my own

failed connection and says, "Here I have a witness,"

and shoves the receiver at me, pointing, "What's that?"

I describe a stranger to a stranger.

The slam-dunk-tall transman strolls past

in a low-cut sequined dress, trailing the coy flutter

of inch-long eyelashes, the slink and sway

of angular hips, and a platinum-teased wig.

Hardly a spectacle in the casino. "See!"

she cries to the woman on the other end,

having lost to this too-much-woman.

Abject Impermanence in Kansas

                    —for Jamie D'Agostino

It wasn't so long ago
Then it was longer than we thought.

Really it was a step or two beyond thinking.

The edge is out there somewhere.
The photograph I'm holding proves it.

Here's another friend who has fallen into a frame
And nowhere else.

In the closet, there's a shoebox holding a wallet-sized
Grand Canyon and the largest ball of string in Kansas.

Immutability was not a dream, then it was.
Now we have nothing and don't care.

Ontologically rich, metaphysically poor,
The sublime non-substance of any living.

Some people die with their boots on, not making it
out of the trenches or even a few feet farther.

Our boots are only muddy.

Anyone can track us down.

We reinvent desertion and call it flight

only to be arrested and fall too easily from the sky.

Be careful which way you point that gun.

We want to see your license for extinction.

Twigs snap, snap again.

Now we're running fast.

The arrhythmia of rumors causes us to stop

And catch a breath.

The canary long ago dead in the deep tunnels

Of our visions. No answer was ever forthcoming.

When the stage was finally reached

No one arrived to play the part.

The horizon pulled back. Curtains in flames.

Cowboys gasp in the dust behind the herd

Headed for Abilene.

The Flint Hills napped into gravel.

A Distant Theory

I'm not much different from the Death Valley rocks
caught on time-lapse video in a penitent migration
across the desert, so slow no horizon shows up
so the rocks declare themselves churches. Altars
of stone where the sun sacrifices eons of light and rips
open a relentless bleeding heat. A once-a-year rain is
rebirth, born again into going nowhere fast.

Not the horizons of religion, but a religion of horizons
that I'm driving into and can see as far as I want
though much of the time my wanting is small
while my longing is long as this interstate. No purple
mountains majesty to distract, to obstruct the view.

I'm driving west and east at once. No one direction
without the other, equal and opposite, and always
caught between. I slip easily, relativity to quantum,
even as the map's names, Ft. Hays, Quinter,
Goodland, tumble west. Near Burlington, grass gone,
a few cows overgraze the bare bushes and drink dust.

Every thirty miles there's a pullover with a plaque
declaring what happened here, or somewhere

near here: a stunned loneliness in the Cathedral
of the Plains, a garden of broken glass, the world's
largest ball of twine, ambush and circling of wagons,
a reminder that there were a few people who stayed
and beat themselves and others senseless,
and there still are a few.

An overlooked Burma Shave sign haunts the roadside
with a clean-shaven narrative cutting close to the wire
fence strung between limestone posts where the rags
of a coyote hang and are picked apart by ceaseless
wind and bullets. Just another body bleeding
in bad light and no salvation for anyone
on this side of the horizon.

Point Dume Screen Test

— for Dorian Heartsong

The sign reads that the promontory is sacred to

the Chumash people, a posted holiness,

a promise yet to keep, a reminder of what was

borrowed and never given back, something more

than the scattered half-buried empty beer bottles,

tar balls, and flaccid condoms shipwrecked at low tide.

This point of rough-risen rock where the beach arcs

 away on either side, as if the dark beak

of a stone bird and its swept back sandy wings

are flying us out over the Pacific, the olive branch of

a promised land still to be brought back, as the tide

slowly pulls open and closed its restless wet curtain.

Windows of hunger open to gulls and sandpipers

who work the shimmer for what's just below

the surface, for what's just out of sight,

as we try to forget whatever we conceived

for ourselves this day and most others.

But for the others, down below and in back of this great

metamorphic bird, cameras work themselves into moist

positions, as the rush of foam works up her thighs,

embraces her hips that are about to set sail,

the gossamer clinging of a white lace dress,
and the upsweeping waves palming the curve
of her breasts that drip back the ocean's attentions,
 while the line of other young women wait their chance
at Point Dume. The surf's hammer works grain by
grain the dissembling, and we want only to believe
and follow the laughter and cries of children running
in and away from the salt surge. Perhaps later,
when they've forgotten or thrown away their plastic
yellow pails and red shovels, what we have
to tell them they will never accept, even if we are sure,
but mostly we want them to believe in this life
and not be dragged down in the undertow of years.

A tailless lizard scurries across rocks covered
with spray-painted initials, names the waves
will later reread along with their fading promises.
Even the flock of bikini-clad young women finished
with the screen test turn away, glad to escape
the Creature of the Black Lagoon for another evening—
not to be pecked clean of their softness by what flies
and crawls past, not to be lost or misplaced
in this vast space fenced by ocean and sky,
not to be deafened by the incessant churning of wind
and dusk, clinging to their lens' suntan resurrections.

The rest of us scrape the black scars of tar
from the soles of our feet, to be left with only
longings, sitting on the edge of blankets or laid back
in the warm sand, working toward becoming
something less than all that we think we once desired.

Motel, Hayti, MO

1

Brass bells ring around their necks, rhythmic
swaying chimes, an odd beginning to time,
an odd end too as rocks shift under the weight
of their hoofs, clatter of stones down steep slopes,
rickety valley percussionists, the slow plodding
of long-haired beasts, horns wrapped with red wool
braids, a flush of enlightenment in the first snow
fall, the first subzero temperatures, and the summit
no longer there. It's only something thought
about yesterday, beards drifted white, crawling
the trail on knees, breathing the last breath again
and again, wringing out the little left, prayer flags
tied the entire length of rope bridges
across chasms above the rush of water a thousand
feet below. There's no turning back,
there's no forward, just the next white step,
where only the raven riding the white squall
tells them they are not paper thin,
even when the clouds are a wrinkled tissue.

2

The land is low and flat and hardly rises
above the water. Frogs croak before sundown,
the noisy hinges between day and night.
I wait too long before driving the main
street through town. I miss the catfish dinner
at Bordeaux Cafe. I miss the barbeque
at Chubby's, closed at eight o'clock.
I follow the sign pointing to
the business district. Nearly unlit,
the central square is not a courthouse
or county seat, but houses fire engines
and a charred darkness.
Around the edges there's Bills Hardware
and Bukowitz's Apparel for Men and next
door Bukowitz's Apparel for Women,
the only stores that flare neon as the rest sink out
of sight into the wide vacancy of river bottomland.

3

The alarm goes off. For a moment I don't remember
where I am. I'm reaching through all that I've lost.
A gray wisp slips through the curtain

and I remember this flatness that is held
blind by fog. Who slept here two nights ago?
I'm working my way down. What mountain
did I climb? Out the window, beyond
the parking lot, the curved-cane-pole, dust-to-dawn
lights flicker off, the fields stagnant,
no place for water to run, it sits in long
parallel pools, glistering furrowed shadows
over drowned crops. The frogs love it
and forget to stop their staccato croaking.
If I could make it to the top of a summit
to the feathering plume of blown snow
rising off a steep slope into pristine sky,
the mountain sighing into a new day,
just like this fog, this vast exhalation
of bottom land, I'd say yes. If the previous
occupants were there already planting
a brightly colored flag, they would be
wrapped in thick layers of water-proof insulation,
wear crampons and mirrored sunglasses
so dark only the flare of sun on snow burns
through, there breathing from an oxygen
bottle in this rarefied air at the door
of their first business appointment,
while I'm still taking a shower.

Geography Bull

The National Geographic arrives in the mail
And under its clear plastic wrap the monthly list,
Five questions, headlined, "Are You a Geo-Genius?"

Little hope here, but has that ever stopped a swagger,
My monthly paltry average of correct guesses 3 out of
5. This does not in any way slow me down

Competing for this honor. I'm looking for a belt buckle
The size of a dinner plate for riding rodeo bulls that
I saw once walking across a diner in Coffeyville, KS.

And the first question twisting out of the arena gate
Is too easy, the name of a Canadian River
That shares a name with a French church famous

In a bloody WWI battle. The poet, Richard Hugo,
Advises, in his essay "Nuts & Bolts," to never answer
A question asked, so I won't. I'm high in the saddle

With one correct unanswered question under my belt.
Question two, though I don't know the answer, I can
Guess, a dead giveaway, asking what country lies

Southeast of Florida that has three thousand islands,
 Islets, and cays, but how many will still be above water
As the planet's fever rises. Of course, that's not

What's asked. Question three requires a triangulation
With three continents to find out which one is
Separated from Antarctica by the Scotia Sea.

Australia is a no go, too far away. Africa just isn't right
With all those great white sharks surfing the beaches.
So South America it is and it is, and so I've aced

Another answer, but there's nothing about
The shrinking ice cap and how much wider every sea
Will be, swelling the distance. Do we even have time

For answers facing such dire foolishness? But I'm up to
Three correct though the brahma is bucking himself
nearly to heaven and off the map. With question four

I can taste victory and it's not steak, this bull will have
None of that. With only two countries filling the Iberian
Peninsula, not counting a reasond'etre symbol

Of an insurance company, maybe the crumbling

Remnants of the Pillars of Hercules, maybe even Scylla

Without Charybdis fame, the original "between a rock

And hard place," but it comes with that giveaway

Direction of the southwestern tip, which is awfully

Near The Rio Tinto where Columbus set sail on

        the ocean

Blue, and you know where that blunder and plunder

got us. Then the last question, which is so easy, I could

Stop thinking and I'd know it, except my secret is some

Old coins with an old colonial country stamped on

Them settled by English wood cutters in the 1630's

Southeast of Mexico. There's no penny for your

Thoughts and it wouldn't be worth a plug nickel any-

way. This month it's just too easy to be a geo-

genuis, but no continent-sized bruises served

on a rodeo belt buckle riding the rodeo circuit.

Real Rumors of Rain

Now that it's done being undone,

or the end of the beginning of undone,

depending on the harrumphing water pumps

and which side of the bulldozer blade

is contemplated, or if a phoenix

can rise from the wet ashes

of flood insurance, now that the poor

replacements for the Ark, johnboats

and helicopters, are docked and landed.

The warnings were of "fire and ice"

not breached levees, though ignored

apocalyptic footnotes after-noted.

Post-Its of black mold crawl up walls,

freely stocking lonely refrigerators,

an unpaid tenant there to guard

against occupancy, not knowing the real monster

of this paved-over estuary is the fungal

underworld, thrilled and thriving on humidity.

Fine films of filaments never heartsick,

heartbroken, or longing for home.

Invincible. How little has changed

in the aftermath of changing light: false starts,

real rumors, the turning back, returning,

as if life is treading light and dancing on rushing water.

Leafing Town

No specific arrangement: oak to maple to oak.
No critical filing: sweet gum to hickory.
Just another smothering, smoldering pile of leaves:

No facsimile nose, nostrils, brow, brown eyes.
My face a leaf on the sidewalk, below the restaurant
Window. Looking up, I can hardly see a thing:

Long wedge of sky between tall buildings.
Wind shifts, I suffer a diminishing imprecision.
What is there to do through a leafy afternoon?

I count the glassy light of windows
Pooling up the walls. Reconfirming
Their changeless ascending numbers.

I could be a pigeon cooing on a high
Lime-stained sill. Not today, even
Their awkward plummeting can't uplift me.

I could be the rusting causeway railing
Above these leaves. Its steel keeps
The occasional pedestrian from falling

Into city traffic. No stopping the jumper.
I'm not stopping myself. My face
Reshuffled blows down the street.

At the curb, in the gutter,
On the sidewalk, at a bus bench,
Tumbling through red light's,

I could have been something.
My mother still thinks so.
My father's a lost leaf.

Don't We Rain

She had some horses she loved.
She had some horses she hated.

These were the same horses.

—Joy Harjo

Don't we all want to love the world?

I want it to be easy and, by wanting, become uneasy.

Even when we are hating, we are loving the world.

You don't believe that do you? What if there is no

world to hate and it is in our hating that creates

this other world, the one we are supposed to love?

Does that mean there is only one world

to love out of this seething cauldron of us

or no world at all as I listen to the ceaseless summer

rain raise river levels and wash nearly everything

away in the river bottoms?

What if there is no possibility of failure? Success una-

voidable, the equal outcome of love and hate. Success,

the blind alley we walk down and down again, and in

our blindness, where we begin to run our hands along

the walls, hoping for the loose brick

that opens the hidden door where we pass through,

and it still conceals a key that belongs to no lock.
We could turn around, turn back, return to where
we ended, not calling it failure but success having
found another way to not exit.

My mother gone beyond gone, her house yet to sell,
so cut down the spruce tree between two tall pin oaks
in the front yard. In the crowning shade, the spruce
leans, a success, but it leans toward failure, falling
or about to fall, declared unaesthetic in
this neighborhood of straight lines. Life's command-
ment: Thou shall cut with words and saw.

It turns out there's not enough fence and not fence
that's high enough to keep a raccoon or cat from climb-
ing the house to the second story eave to destroy a
phoebe nest, leaving the mother to call all morning and
afternoon, for its mate, for it's just hatched brood, for a
world beyond love, hate, but not beyond loss.

At the dinner table, each spooned failure, each forked
failure, each failure of words, a celebration of failure,
whether in love or hate. This the paradox,
their state of memory a monumental abyss,
cast in a bronze evening light to nothing

that has happened in that immeasurable moment

when the present is ground to dust between

the millstones of the past and future.

The future of the past, the silence of the past,

both a crumbling edifice of grief.

Why a city when one room of sadness

in a house of regret is all we need?

Now there is no forgetting, no water to drink

and wash it down: the Cuyahoga fired,

the deserted Aral Sea, Glacier's glaciers gone.

Don't we all want to love the world?

ABOUT THE POET

Walter Bargen has published 23 books of poetry. Recent books include: *Days Like This Are Necessary: New & Selected Poems* (BkMk Press, 2009), *Trouble Behind Glass Doors* (BkMk Press, 2013), *Perishable Kingdoms* (Grito del Lobo Press, 2017), *Too Quick for the Living* (Moon City Press, 2017), *My Other Mother's Red Mercedes* (Lamar University Press, 2018). His work has appeared in over 300 magazines. His awards include: a National Endowment for the Arts Fellowship, Chester H. Jones Foundation Award, and the William Rockhill Nelson Award. He was appointed the first poet laureate of Missouri (2008-2009). www.walterbargen.com

THE BOOKS BY WALTER BARGEN

Fields of Thenar (Singing Wind Press, 1980)

Mysteries in the Public Domain (BkMk Press, UMKC, 1990)

Yet Other Waters (Timberline Press, 1990)

The Vertical River (Timberline Press, 1995)

Rising Water: Reflections on the Year of the Great Flood (Pe-kitanoui Publications, 1994)

At The Dead Center Of Day (BkMk Press, UMKC, 1997)

Water Breathing Air (Timberline Press, 1999)

Harmonic Balance (Timberline Press 2001)

Vow of Hunger (Snark Publishing, 2003)

The Body of Water (Timberline Press, 2003)

The Feast (BkMk Press-UMKC, 2004)

Remedies for Vertigo (WordTech Press, 2006)

West of West (Timberline Press, 2007)

Theban Traffic (WordTech Press, 2008)

Days Like This Are Necessary: New & Selected Poems (BkMk Press-UMKC, 2009), *Endearing Ruins/Liebenswerte Ruinen* (Liliom – Verlag, 2012)

Trouble Behind Glass Doors (BkMk Press-UMKC, 2013)

Gone West/Ganz im Westen (Liliom – Verlag, 2014)

Quixotic (Timberline Press, 2014)

Three-Corner Catch (Timberline Press, 2015)

Perisable Kingdoms (Timberline Press, 2017)

Too Quick for the Living (Moon City Press, 2017)

My Other Mother's Red Mercedes (Lamar University Press, 2018)

RECENT BOOKS FROM SINGING BONE PRESS

A Hermit Has No Plural by Gabor Gyukic

My God, How Many Mistakes I've Made by Endre Kukorelly (translated from Hungarian by Gabor Gyukic and Michael Castro)

How Things Stack Up by Michael Castro

Two Gardens: Modern Hebrew Poems of the Bible (Poems by twenty-four Israeli poets translated by Jeff Friedman and Nati Zohar)

Poems from the Buddha's Footprint by Sunthorn Phu (translated from Thai by Noh Anothai)

Double Identity by Allison Joseph

Doubled Radiance: Poetry and Prose of Li Qingzhao (translated from Chinese by Karen An-Hwei Lee)

We Need to Talk: New and Selected Poems by Michael Castro

The Heart Attacks of the Soul: Gypsy Cantos by Attila Balogh (translated from Hungarian by Gabor Gyukic and Michael Castro)

Butter in a Jar: Days in the Life of Iola Thomas by Jerred Metz

Uncle Duke Gathers His Wits: Truths and Heresies by W. K. Haydon

The Angel of Mons: A World War I Legend by Jerred Metz

The Melody Lingers: New and Selected Poems by Shlomo Vinner

Made in the USA
Lexington, KY
20 December 2019